This book belongs to:

_____

_____

_____

EAT THE RAINBOW
shine like the sun

WRITTEN BY
HAILEY BATCHELOR

ILLUSTRATED BY ALLIE SASSA
PRODUCTION BY STEPHEN BATCHELOR

LET'S EXPLORE TOGETHER,
THIS COLORFUL ARRAY,
DISCOVER HEALTHY GROWING FOODS,
TO EAT EVERY DAY.

FROM BRIGHT REDS TO SOOTHING BLUES,
THE RAINBOW OF FOOD
OFFERS SO MUCH GOODNESS
FOR ME AND FOR YOU!

RED KEEPS OUR HEART
HEALTHY AND STRONG,

WHEN YOU TAKE A BITE,
YOU'LL FEEL ENERGIZED ALL DAY LONG!

ORANGE IS FULL OF VITAMIN A
WHICH KEEPS YOUR EYES
SPARKLING BRIGHT,

MUNCH ON ORANGE
FOR SUPER-DUPER SIGHT!

YELLOW FOOD HELPS OUR BODY HEAL
OUCHIES AND CUTS,

LIKE SUNSHINE ON A PLATE,
BRINGING STRENGTH THAT STRUTS!

GREEN FOOD HELPS OUR BODY
FIGHT OFF SICK GERMS,

MAKING US HEALTHY SUPERHEROES,
WHO ARE READY TO LEARN.

BLUE FOODS HELP KEEP OUR BRAIN
STRONG AND HEALTHY,

FROM BLUEBERRIES TO GRAPES,
THEY MAKE OUR MINDS
BRIGHT AND STEALTHY!

PURPLE FOODS KEEP OUR
TUMMIES HAPPY,
OUR BRAINS TOO!

FIGS AND PLUMS,
SO YUMMY AND TRUE.

OUR ADVENTURE'S DONE,
THE SUN'S GOING DOWN,
BUT REMEMBER THE MAGIC
WE'VE FOUND ALL AROUND.

EACH RAINBOW COLOR,
A FOOD THAT WILL GLEAM,
SHINING LIKE YOU AND ME,
HELPING US BEAM!

NOW, MY FRIENDS,
YOU'VE LEARNED THE WAY,
FILL YOUR PLATES WITH COLOR,
EVERY SINGLE DAY.

THESE VIBRANT FOODS
WILL MAKE YOU SHINE,
JUST LIKE THE SUN, YOU AND I!

STARS TWINKLE ABOVE,
IT'S TIME TO SAY GOODBYE,
I'LL BE HERE,
BRINGING WARMTH FROM THE SKY.
KEEP SHINING, LITTLE ONES,
DAY AND NIGHT,
NOURISH WITH RAINBOWS,
FEEL HEALTHY, HAPPY, AND BRIGHT.

For all inquiries please visit
www.efflorescencehealth.com

Made in the USA
Las Vegas, NV
26 September 2024